For the Love of Turbo

By
Angela Chesher

ISBN: 978-1074029623

This story is dedicated to our fur-baby Turbo, who was diabetic but because of his love and strength to live, inspired me to write about his memory. To my husband, my family and friends, because of their love and support for me to never give up and to keep trying, because with God's love all things are possible.

I also have to include our other fur-babies Buster, Ben, Rachel and Maggie who got me through some very sad days. Because of all the people and pets in my life, they have made me a better person. I would also like to include my friend Kathy Pearson who helped me write this story. She saw the beauty in my heart and helped it come to life in this story.

Thank you all so very much.

God Bless,
Angela

A Little About Me!

As long as I can remember I have always cared about animals. When I was young, I brought home stray dogs, pregnant cat's, and baby ducks. Yes, a baby duck. And I wanted it so bad. Knowing I had to convince my Mom was another story. So, when I showed her how cute it was, I told her *it won't be any trouble*, and of course added *I'll take care of it...* She shrewdly said if it doesn't poop on the floor, I could keep it. Really?? This was going to be easy. But as soon as I set it down... poop, poop everywhere. So needless to say, I didn't get to keep the duck. Hmm, how did she know it was going to poop on the floor???

In all my many attempts to have a pet, any pet of my own, I never really succeeded in convincing my parents to let me keep any of the critters I found. But that didn't change my love for animals. I made friends with them at every opportunity... even if it had to be the squirrels in our backyard. Or sometimes, we would visit my grandparents and that was heaven.

They lived in the hills of Kentucky and I have great memories of going up to the top of the holler where it was quiet and green and filled with butterflies. There was no television, no computers or cell phones, but there was a crystal clear 'crick' to run barefoot through and there was always something to do. But most importantly to me, there were plenty of animals!!

My grandpa had a mule he used for plowing but as a friend that mule was a bad boy. That mule was not very friendly and he was a little scary. His business was to plow, not be my friend, and he let me know that in his mulish way. There were a lot of chickens I could feed scraps to but chickens are not very cuddly. So, I tried to make friends with the two dogs. Do you know country dogs are good at hunting but not so good at keeping a little girl entertained? Thankfully I had some cousins who lived there too and our summers were filled with fun and mischief.

I remember one time my sis and older cousins were picking on us smaller ones so I covered up some chicken poop with a little bit of dirt and asked my sister to come over real close. Then it happened... squish!! Right between her toes, needless to say I ran and ran and ran!!

I hope everyone has such a place in their past to cling to as an adult. Maybe not catching lighting bugs or running through cricks but fun times with family and friends. I would hope however; you don't have any memories of old smelly outhouses. Oh yeah, my grandparents had one of those too. My first time in there was a real eye opener.

As I was sitting there looking around and trying not to think of the smell, I wondered where the toilet paper was. I glanced over and saw a JC Penney's catalog. It was not for shopping or to pass the time. I remembered what my grandma said… pull out a page and rub it as soft as you can get it!! Although it never got very soft, this memory now has a tender spot in my heart. It has a lot softer place in my heart than it did on by bottom!

Of course, times have changed and it has altered the holler I remember. The porch where I snapped beans with my grandma is no longer there. A newer house has been built with indoor plumbing, the mule is no longer needed for plowing and the early morning howling of the hunting dogs is silent. There is no longer a rooster crowing or the warm soft feeling of the feather bed. Or, the smell of my grandma frying bacon and making huge homemade biscuits, as big as saucers, we always dipped in chocolate cocoa syrup. Memories. Sometimes that is what sustains us.

So, I hope you enjoy the journey I will take you on in telling my story about an amazing dog named Turbo. There's also a little bit about each of us including Rachel, Buster, Ben and Maggie because they are an important part of our lives. But no matter what your feelings are after reading this, I hope you love your pets and treat them like family. They deserve it. We all know that when someone, even a pet, is no longer in your life you can't say I love you, kiss them goodnight or wrap your arms around them. But it will be the memories you have made that will help you get through the loss. Well that, and for me, the love of God.

The House in the Holler

The Beginning

They say it is hard to start your life over when you are stuck in a rut for years and accepting the road you are on. I have to agree. I did that same thing myself. I always wanted a family and a home and to find someone I could trust and build my life with. But the dreams I had hoped for did not happen for me, at least not in the beginning.

First, I married too young. I chose not to listen to anyone's advice, because I thought I knew everything and I thought I was in love. Second, I married too young. I wish I had listened to my mom's advice but I didn't. I had to make my own mistakes and I had to live with them. It turned out the mistakes I made cost me my self-esteem and my confidence. At least for a season.

It all started in Arizona where I met my first husband and thought I was going to live my fairy tale dream. But reality slapped me right in the face and I lived a quiet, lonely life. He had been married before and was much older than me. I could not go anywhere for a long period of time without checking in. In ignorance I freely handed over my paychecks and let him make all the decisions regarding our money, bills, purchases, everything.

Oh, I admit I was young and I was trusting but that was not always in my best interests. Assuming his age and experience would cover our needs was very naïve. So, I allowed the loss of my home, pets and almost my life because I had no confidence in myself and I relinquished all control instead of sharing the burden.

But I kept hanging on, I thought it was the right thing to do. Our wedding vows said for better or worse. Well just when I had the nerve to tell him I was not happy he said he wanted to move to Las Vegas and start fresh. But nothing changed once we moved to Las Vegas.

I had to leave my dog Bandit behind because he told me the new apartment didn't take dogs. I was heart-broken and didn't want to go. But once again I let my insecurity get to me and I gave in. When we moved into the new place, I found out they did accept pets. But that required an extra deposit. If I had known this, I would have made sure all of my furry kids made the move with us. Well, I had taken my cat Tiger so now I would have to keep her out of sight or pay the deposit. I chose to pay the deposit so at least I would have my kitty.

Later on, I think his guilt about Bandit got to him a little and he let me rescue a dog named Tuxedo. It broke my heart that someone wanted to put him to sleep because he had an ear infection. Please if you get a pet, take care of them. They count on you. But if you can't, give them to a shelter or another family so they will have a loving home.

Then one day I reached a crisis point. I got tired of my years of feeling inadequate. I finally became tired of not being good enough. I quit believing I would become fat or that I was ugly and I started believing someone else would want me. Someone who would love me for who I was. And I began to believe I could take care of myself, on my own. I didn't really need to be unhappy. I hated living with the threat of eviction because I never knew how our money was being spent. Looking back, the biggest mistake I made was allowing behavior that had destruction written all over it. There is a saying that you have to hit rock bottom before you will change your life. Well let me tell you, I hit it hard and it almost killed me.

I was so embarrassed and upset with myself for wasting my life with someone who did not respect me. But I allowed it. Oh, he told me… he *loved* me. But I finally figured out… if someone loves you, why would they treat you this way? What had I done? Was it my fault? Was I allowing him and the devil to defeat me? On my lowest day I remember going to the bathroom and opening the medicine cabinet and looking at the pills that were there. I had no idea what they were, but I didn't care.

I opened some of the vials and got a glass of water and stood in the hallway crying uncontrollably. I was asking God to help me, show me something please, to give me strength. Please God, please. But I didn't hear anything and I started sliding down the wall till my head was on my knees. Then I felt a cold nose on my arm. It was my little Tuxedo.

I looked in his eyes and the love I saw from him made me realize I was loved and needed by my pets Tuxedo and Tiger. So, I hugged his neck and thanked him for saving me. I believe that God sent him to my side that day to show me I was loved. To let me know God was watching over me. And that a love from a dog was all I needed to get up and make that decision to get out forever!!!

I know now that thinking about suicide is not to be taken lightly. I also know there is always someone who will be there for you. Embarrassed or not, I could have called my Mother, or my Dad, or my friend Teresa. I may not have liked what they said, but they would have been there for me. They would have told me, my life matters. Your life matters. Change can be a good thing but you have to find the strength to make different choices.

I found a place to go to, but I was not able to take Tuxedo. He was placed in a home with kids and I was told he was happy. So, my cat Tiger and me, started our new lives together. I look back now on that time in my life as a very big lesson. I learned what I really deserved and the way I should be loved. I learned I had to forgive my ex-husband in order to move on. I also learned that was not easy but I could not live in the past.

I saw that God was there with me through all the heartache and sadness because there were times that the outcome could have been different. But God had a plan for me and I know now that I had to go through the stinky stuff to reveal the fresh new days ahead of me. I would have to rebuild my trust, open my heart to love again, and learn to respect myself. I eventually did learn that life was about growing into the person God wants us to be. I finally met my current husband and all the wonderful pets that I would have in my life… and of course the reason for this story, my Turbo.

Life Goes On

Moving on after my divorce was *plenty* scary. I had to find a better, full time job, to pay my bills. A co-worker at my part-time job told me about an opening at a very famous hotel on the strip. Of course, everyone knew it was once owned by a mobster!!! It was really neat because we got to go through some of the hidden passages that come out in another hotel!!

I worked grave yard and swing shifts and that was a hard adjustment for me. But thankfully I had also learned you do what is necessary to survive. These changes in my life made it easy to also go through a period of doubt. I was very alone and of course feeling sorry for myself. Should I go back to my Ex? I could have gone to live with either my Dad or my Mom, even my sister offered. And although I did not mean to hurt anyone's feelings, I knew I needed to own up to my own mistakes.

I told them thank you… but no… and just kept going on. I made some new mistakes along the way, being so naïve and not very experienced. But things were about to change for me.

Before I got the hotel job, when I was working part-time in a card shop in Las Vegas, there was a guy that would come in and clean the windows every week. He was tall, blonde, handsome and yes, he had a nice tush! When I would see him come in to get paid, I would go in the back and hide. I was still shy about meeting or talking to people. I really was not ready to get back in a relationship. I still didn't feel pretty or that I deserved to be happy. Besides, who would want me?

The girls would tease me after he left. They would say he asked 'where was the girl with the pretty blue eyes'!! I just smiled and left it at that. It was good to have the support of my co-workers around me but it took me some time to realize I did deserve to be happy and to be loved.

Anyway, I had started my new job at the hotel and since I didn't work at the card shop, I didn't see the window cleaner anymore. One day I got the courage to go in and ask the girls at the card shop for his phone number. I told them I needed a window cleaner for someone else because I didn't think it was any of their business to know it was for me. I guess what I really thought was that I didn't want to feel dumb if he shot me down.

I must have dialed his phone number what felt like a hundred times. But as soon as I heard the ring tone, I would always hang up. I finally just bit the bullet and let it ring. Well, here goes nothing! When he answered his voice sounded so nice it made it easier to get the courage to speak. I said 'Hi' and we had a short conversation before he said, 'I'm not trying to be a jerk but who are you????'

My mouthed dropped and I almost hung up. But somehow, I stumbled on to say, 'the girl with the blue eyes you always asked about at the card shop.'

Nothing. Silence. Did he hang up? I knew this would happen. Why would he remember me? Then like music to my ears, he said 'oh it's you'. He told me he had plans but would like to give me a call so we can get together. Really? Yeah!! Yippeeee!! Happy Dance!!

But I acted cool. I'm not sure how I did that but I said that would be nice, made sure he had my phone number, and said 'bye'. Of course, I thought it would be days before he would call. It wasn't days. Two days later we had plans to meet at his house and start our date. I wanted to drive my own car in case I got there and he was a jerk. He gave me directions and said when you come in to the housing development, make a left turn, and it's the third house on the left.

Okay, no problem. I got this. Well... of course, I turned in and made a *right*. Then I realized I had made a wrong turn. All I could think about was please don't let him be outside waiting. No such luck. There he was grinning from ear to ear. You could tell he was ready to say something, oh darn.

I pulled in the driveway and before I could get all of the way out of my car, he said. 'What happened? Did you have a blonde moment??'

Any other time, from things said to me in the past, I would have just run to my car and got in and left. But there was something in me that would not let my nerves get the best of me. What came out of my mouth was. 'Yeah I did. Got a problem with that??'

But it was said with a smile and a grin from ear to ear just like him. He smiled and said he was glad I had a sense of humor. I remember before going in the house, he said there's two things that he wanted me to know, so we don't waste each other's time. I said okay, and he said… 'I won't get married again and my dog has to like you.' Well on the marriage issue I was not even ready for that and the dog was no problem. I love animals and they love me!

We got inside and as I sat down, I looked out of his sliding door to the back yard and there sat Buster. My heart sank, he was a chow mix and looked like he was ready to eat me for dinner. Ted asked if I was ready to meet Buster. I said *suuure.* I was sitting on the couch as he opened the door and it was like something from a movie. With a little foam dangling from his mouth he ran straight at me. Thankfully he came to a sudden stop in front of me. I put my hand out to let him take a whiff and well… wouldn't you know it? He let me pet him! Ted's face was in shock. He told me that Buster is not fond of too many people. Okay, that went well for me!

He changed the subject, 'are you hungry? How about McDonald's?'

I really didn't care what we ate. Fast food, dog food, anything would be okay. Luckily what I said was *sure*

again. So off we went. But instead of the golden arches, we ended up at Planet Hollywood on the strip. I had a wonderful time. We talked and laughed and it was fun. I really had fun!

After dinner we both wanted to wander through the mall where we had had dinner because we were enjoying each other's company so much and neither of us wanted the evening to end. I was not paying much attention and I brushed up against his arm and our hands touched. Ted reached out and took my hand. And even though he said he would not get married again, at that moment I believed he would be my husband and best friend someday.

When I moved in with Ted, I was able to bring my cat Tiger with me. Ted was allergic to cats but he liked Tiger so much and Buster and her got along so well, that he would just wash his hands after petting her and it worked out. We were both a little nervous being in a new relationship, but we both never brought up our pasts because you can't change it, just learn from it. And we both don't judge people for their lives because if you have never walked in their shoes you really don't know the reason for their choices in life.

So, life was good. He worked all day at his window cleaning, and I worked at my hotel job on the strip. I worked grave yard and swing and that was hard to adjust to. We hardly saw each other, so I would get home and go with him sometimes just to ask how his day was and so we could spend time with each other.

But we managed and things were good. I think I was still very insecure so I worried about a lot of things. I worried that his parents wouldn't like me. They lived in Sacramento California but I still spent too much time worrying about meeting them. I would talk on the phone with Lia and Milt and they seemed nice. But talking to them on the phone was safe. It was when they told me they had decided to make a special trip to Las Vegas to meet me that the panic set in.

I was so scared. But when we went to see them at an RV park, where they were staying in their motor home, they came out smiling excitedly and hugged and hugged us. They even had gifts for us…gifts for Ted… and gifts for me! It was amazing. I felt so special and of course I got to meet their dog Barney. How perfect that they loved animals just like me! It was wonderful that we all got along so well. It was nice to have good people in my life.

But life is full of the opportunity to worry. My mom called to say that she and Carl, my stepfather, wanted to move back to Kentucky. I wouldn't be able to just drive a few hours to see them anymore. I would have to take extra time off work and drive for days… or take a plane. Both options would be expensive. I wouldn't see my mom, my best friend, as often as I had been. To me it seemed like she was moving to another country, it might as well be Timbuktu. I knew that was just my insecurity and that she would be happier closer to our family in Kentucky.

However, before they left, they wanted to meet Ted. Conversations with him on the phone could only relieve so much of their concern for me. Parents worry too. So, they came to see us. I especially wanted Ted to meet Carl. My stepfather was a good man. He was the kind of man I had hoped to find to love me. He loved my mom unconditionally and treated her like a queen. I think I wanted Ted to see their relationship because it was the example I clung to. It was what I needed. I needed to be loved and to have commitment in my life.

As a child I loved my father *as a child* does, without reservations. I thought he was the best, my hero… but I saw him through the eyes of a child. As an adult I can see that as a husband my view of what to expect was a little clouded. Was he supportive of my mother? I knew they argued a lot and I didn't see a lot of physical affection. He is still my father and I love him but I wish my example of who to marry had been different. I wish I had expected more and not settled for less than what I knew later was so much better.

When my mother and Carl met Ted and saw that I was living in a cute house, in a good neighborhood, and that I had a life with my beloved pets, they were so relieved. They knew Ted was a hard worker and that we both had stable jobs. To say my Mom was glad to see that I was in a better relationship and that I was happy…

is an understatement. She was glad I had met my true love. They finally felt free to move to Kentucky. They knew I would be okay.

But as the months went by, I was trying to work through my concerns about our relationship. I was happy with Ted but was it going to move to another level? A level that might include marriage? We talked about marriage sometimes but… it seemed our past wounds had made us both very guarded. I couldn't deny Ted had told me up front that he wouldn't get married again. I also couldn't deny that for me, this was no longer a very comforting thought.

One day I remember having a strange conversation with his mom. She asked me if I would marry Ted, if he asked me to. I was cautious when I told her I would because I was wondering why she was asking me this particular question. Strange. I thought it was strange.

My birthday was just around the corner and I love, love, love birthday's!!! It was funny when a few days after this conversation with his mother, Ted told me Lia and Milt were coming for a visit and they wanted to take us out to dinner. I didn't have enough notice to get the time off from my work so I arranged to meet them on my dinner break.

It was good to see them but it was a little strange that they immediately started talking about going to Hawaii in April. Well, I'll have you know; I had never been anywhere except Kentucky and Arizona and

Hawaii sounded very beautiful and romantic. Then wham! Seemingly out of nowhere, Lia asked if I would like to go too?

What me??? I looked at Ted and he was grinning from ear to ear! I said yes of course. The first thing I did when I got back to work was see my boss for the time off. She said she would work it out for me to go and I was going to Hawaii!!! To me, this was like dream, a once-in-a-lifetime thing. I couldn't wait to call my mom to tell her. Me, Angie…her daughter, was going to Hawaii! She was so happy for me.

All day while we were getting ready to leave for the airport Ted was so nervous and going to the bathroom A LOT!! I thought he was afraid of flying. Even at the airport, he was checking out their bathroom! I was worried but he said he was fine.

His parents were already in Hawaii so they got our rooms with them so we didn't have to worry about that. I was *sooo* excited and wanted a window seat. These days I need an aisle seat because I have to… would you believe it… check out their bathroom all the time! But on this great adventure I wanted to see everything. We got to our seats and I sat down and Ted got up to look in the overhead compartment and sat down again. A few minutes later he got up and did it again.

They said over the intercom for everyone to be seated, fasten your seatbelts, and off we flew! We asked for the complimentary water and peanuts and

23

Ted got up again and this time when he opened the overhead a piece of rolled up paper fell out. I reached over and looked at it, and he grabbed it and his face looked frustrated.

I asked what it was and he said… here it's for you. On the front he had written "Happy Birthday with all my love, Bun Boy." That's the nickname I had given him, well… he has a nice behind.

I opened it up and it was a beautiful ring. I started crying and told him I didn't deserve such a beautiful ring. And the look on his face was so serious. He told me he wanted me to spend the rest of my life with him. But I was very excited as you can imagine. Ted was also nervous… as you can imagine… so he didn't actually say the words… will you marry me? I started crying again. I thought… oh my gosh, he's going to ask me to marry him. But nothing… I sat beside him on that flight waiting. The fact he had just asked me… I just didn't get… the poor guy.

It was a nice flight but confusing to me. We made it to Hawaii and as soon as I saw his parents, I said look, I got a ring from Ted! I didn't pick up on this at the time but his mom asked me why I was wearing it on my right hand? See, Ted told her he was going to ask me so I guess she was confused too. I didn't even answer her. I just hugged them and was happy to be there.

Wow, was Maui beautiful! Our adjoining room was beautiful too with the ocean was right outside our room.

They had balloons and food for my birthday and I met his step-sister who lived in Hawaii and had helped plan everything. On the hotel grounds there was a lanai used for entertainers and we could see it from our room. In fact, the sliding door in our room was open and I had been maneuvered to it so the singer performing could call me down onto the stage. I was so surprised. I went down to the stage and they sang Happy Birthday! It was a wonderful day. But it was even better later… when I finally got up my nerve to ask Ted what his ring meant.

His response was… I want you to be in my life forever. I want you to please marry me. I was happy he didn't change his mind after the way I reacted… or maybe after the way I hadn't reacted… Thankfully he knew what I had gone through in my past and how uncertain I was so he allowed me grace to be so dense. I hugged him so hard and kissed him and that was the best birthday ever!

The whole trip was amazing and a blur because I was so excited to be there and to have gotten engaged. We both decided to have a year engagement so we would not stress and could save for the wedding. We wanted to enjoy the whole process since I didn't have this before. I told my Dad and my Mom and they were both happy for us. So onward home to plan a wedding and a new chapter in my life!

A New Chapter

It was exciting to plan a wedding. I didn't want a big wedding or a lot of people. I just wanted my family and a small group of friends to be there. I had no idea where we were going to have it until one day I was talking to Ted's mom and she made a suggestion of having it at their house in Shingle Springs, California. It could be an outdoor wedding in their beautiful backyard. I was so touched and happy that she would open up their home for us on our special day.

Since his parents lived in California, Ted and I made a trip up to Lake Tahoe, to get our Marriage License. We spent the entire day up there with his family. They had fireworks over the lake and it was all a part of this wonderful dream. The next day we went to Shingle Springs and took a few days to look at food venues and flowers. To me this was like a fairy tale only in this story… this time, I was the princess.

We went back home to Las Vegas and went on with our regular routine. I wanted to have everything in order for our wedding and not make last minute decisions. So, I called my dad to make sure he could fly out and give me away. I was worried he may not be able to get away from work. I told him I would understand if he was not able to come.

He said there was no way he was going to miss my wedding. He also wanted to take care of my dress, the flowers and the photographer. I didn't want to take advantage of his kindness so I was very prudent in my choices. I got invitations from the card shop where I used to work. That saved me a lot of money. My dress was from a sale at a bridal boutique. The food and the music were a gift from his Mom and step-father. What I enjoyed the most about my wedding was planning and helping his Mom with all the choices.

The big day arrived and we picked up my dad from the airport. My Maid of Honor had also flown out from Tucson, Arizona. The night before the wedding… with all our family and friends… we had a lovely rehearsal dinner. It was so heartwarming to see all the people there who loved us and wanted to share in our special day. Of course, all this happiness made me cry.

We were having our wedding outside so we had to decorate at the very last minute. After the rehearsal dinner we all pitched in to get everything set up. Ted's Mom was worried that all the wild animals might have a field day. They had foxes, raccoons, deer, squirrels and other nocturnal friends that she hoped would not get sick if they tried to eat our decorations!

But when we woke up it was to a beautiful blue sky. There was no wind and not a thing out of place. Now tell me that's not a God thing!! The guests had arrived and I was waiting with my dad to hear the music start. I started to go a little too soon and my dad touched my arm and said not yet little darling and I started to cry. My dad said he was proud of me and I looked beautiful and he knew I was going to be okay.

And the rest was amazing. It was hard to say good bye to everyone when we left on our honeymoon but I was so excited to begin this new chapter in my life. Of course, it was hard getting back to normal routine after being gone for the honeymoon. But you have to pay the bills… so back to work.

Not long after that we settled into our new life, our cat Tiger stopped eating and drinking. I took her to the vet and he ran some tests and said she was starting to have kidney issues. I asked was she in pain and he said not at this time and that I could give her fluids by an IV to keep her hydrated.

I started giving her IV's everyday for a couple of weeks and she just kept getting worse. Tiger was a strong cat, she would let me put the IV in and even if I did it wrong, she never moved, like she knew I was trying to help her.

But in the end, I had to put her to sleep. I had never been through that before and it was the hardest thing for me to do. I cried so much, but I had to be thankful she lived thirteen years and she was not hurting anymore.

I told myself I didn't want any more animals but I was glad I still had Buster. As you know from the cover of this book…. that didn't last. But it wasn't Turbo who entered our lives at this time. About a year after Tiger passed, I missed her so much but I still didn't want to think about getting another cat. I remember one day as we were in our work van, Ted looked over at me and saw tears running down my cheeks. He asked me what was wrong. I didn't even realize I was crying, but I told him I was thinking about Tiger. He mysteriously told me he had a stop to make. Then I noticed we were in front of the animal shelter. I was so upset, but he said… let's just look. Look? Yeah, right. Okay, but no cat!!

Well, meet Maggie.

Maggie

I guess somewhere in my heart I wanted to look, but then I didn't, then I did, so I told him I only wanted a girl with short hair, no male cats. He said okay and we went inside. It's always so hard for me to go in these places because I just wanted to take them all home. And when you read, *dumped off*, *owner has passed no family member wants them*, its breaks my heart. I have all my pets listed in our will so they all have homes to go to in case something happened to Ted and I both at the same time. I pray that people will do this for their pets, who have loved them and been their companion through their life.

Of course, I saw nothing but male cats and long-haired females so I was doing okay. I said to Ted… it's time to go, but as I was going out, I noticed a room off to the side and I asked one of the volunteers if we could go in there. Of course, they said, it's just when we get so many animals, it's an extra room. I said thank you and went in to look around real fast. But as I was walking away, I noticed in a corner there was a cage. Inside this cage was a very quiet cat. She was not making a noise. She was a small beautiful gray and white cat. She was leaning against the cage bars looking at me with her beautiful green eyes.

I asked the girl if I could see her and she said of course! As I started to get closer to the cage her little arms came out from between the bars in the cage, and when it was opened, she just put them around my neck and it was all over!! I started crying. Ted was crying, and even the young girl was crying. And that was that. I'm so thankful Ted took me that day, but I believe God had me notice that room, I still don't know what made me look back, but I'm so glad that I did.

Maggie is still here at the age of twenty-one years old and going strong. She sleeps with me, lays in my lap at night when I'm on our computer, or at any other time she can capture my attention. There have been times people have thought they heard a baby saying 'mama' in the back ground while I was on the phone. No, I would say, that's just my cat, my little girl, my four-legged child, Maggie.

The Move

After bringing Maggie home, I was not too worried about Buster meeting her for the first time. He had been around Tiger so I thought he would adjust fine. However, how would Maggie handle Buster? No worries she just went up to him and he smelled her, turned his back and walked off. He did look a little perturbed, but all went well. She wanted to sleep with him but he was not having any of that, so I was her person and that was okay with me.

Work was still going strong, we were so busy and with it just being the two of us, it made for very long days. But we love what we do, and we have so many wonderful clients who are very loyal and some have become friends. But Las Vegas was getting so many new people and the building was out of control. And the traffic and the cost of living was getting much higher. But I never thought I would ever move.

I loved my home. It was just right and we had beautiful grass and trees. And my neighborhood was safe. No really! At that time, I felt safe there and we didn't have the water issues like they do now so we had green all around us.

So, when Ted started talking about moving to Lake Havasu City, Arizona, I was like... are you crazy??? We had a small vacation home in Parker Arizona. Okay, it was a small trailer but we went there to get away from the hustle of Vegas so it counts. When we visited from time to time to get away from work, we traveled the two and a half hours through desert... and lots of rocks, lots of dry dusty rocks, to get there. There was no green, unless it was in the spring time and you counted the orange blooms of the Ocotillo and the purple scorpion weed. I am sure I never wanted, or even thought of, living anywhere near the place.

But I knew Ted was not happy in Las Vegas. A friend said to him one day... 'hey you have a place in Parker but you have always wanted to live in Lake Havasu City, so why don't you just move there??' Some friend. I stalled for time. I told Ted I needed to go to Lake Havasu and see if we could survive there. We would have to start a new business. We had built up our business in Las Vegas and it had been hard. How would we make it in a small town?

Well, Ted took me up on this. Off we go to Lake Havasu City for a week. On the way into town there was a sign that said a mall was coming, Ted looked at me with excitement and said, 'see there will be shopping coming here soon.' What neither of us knew was that 'soon' in Havasu is a relative term.

I didn't shop a lot in Las Vegas but I do love to walk

around and look at everything. I'm a thrift store, garage sale, antique looking kind of person. I love getting something and fixing it up, it makes me feel good. But I thought, well that's something, I guess. We looked around town but all I could think of was… I don't think I want to live here. I don't do well in the heat and it gets even hotter here than it does in Vegas. As I looked around there were a few cute shops on main street, they even had a Kmart, a movie theater and a beautiful English village. I had heard that at Christmas time it was decorated with lights and they had a boat parade. This was helping Ted but I had to put my big girls pants on. So, I sought a higher authority. I prayed that if it's *meant* to be, God will let it happen. He would have to make a way for our house to sell and even our business. I thought I didn't have a thing to worry about, God has his work cut out for Him!

You have to remember this was in late 1999, so things in Havasu have changed and grown since then. But that week as I saw the look on his face and the excitement building, I caved in. I offered a bone. I said we can try and sell our house and the business when we get home. I know, why did I give in? I really didn't want to move there. But… well, I was pretty sure that selling our house *and* our business were a huge ace up my sleeve. Obviously, I was way too smug.

When we got home, Ted called a realtor who we knew and she came out and looked at the house. Of course, she said that it's in really *hot* neighborhood and there should be no problem selling it. What??? No, no, no...okay, we'll see.

We were coming home from work a few days later and as we drove in, I saw the For-Sale sign in the yard. This was happening, we were selling our home. The home in which we had started our lives together. Could this really be happening? Maybe Ted will change his mind? At least there was still our great business we had to sell. Soooo, the next weekend we went to Lake Havasu to look for homes. On the way there we got a call from our realtor saying we had an offer on the house for full asking price. What?!! It's only been on the market for a few weeks.

My heart sank, but I had to move on and accept what I had agreed to. We found a realtor in Lake Havasu, but we really had to find something and fast. Ted was like, we can stay in our small trailer in Parker. Oh, I don't think so! No way! We are here to work not play every day. So onward for the search of our new home. I was almost about to give I up, when our realtor pulled into the drive of a possibility. There was only one house across the street so it was nice and quiet.

I walked in and saw potential, it had a fireplace, a fenced yard for Buster, and it had a lake view which we lost later on, but it would work. The lady from across the street came over to let us know that all the cars were not hers they were her kid's friends. After we moved in, she told us she did that because we were the first set of people that looked nice. I liked her the moment I met her and she became a wonderful friend and Turbo's second mom. We put in an offer and went back to Las Vegas. Ted contacted a person who was also a window cleaner. Yes, *of course*, he was very interested in buying our business. We worked with him and introduced him to our customers in the next two weeks and he removed the last obstacle to Ted's plan. The move was on. It was official.

As I started packing, I looked around and I had to sit down and think how fast everything had happened. It was so scary but when I think back, I can see that God had a plan to help us get through all of this. Not too much longer after we moved to Lake Havasu, the housing market in Las Vegas took a hard hit. I do believe that if I hadn't listened to God and taken this chance at a new chapter in our lives, I don't know where Ted and I would have ended up. A lot of the business customers we had were closing up, cutting back, and the new owner was much more flexible in the type of work he would take on. He didn't mind working on the big casino jobs that Ted and I avoided.

I really don't like moving. Does anyone like it? It is the time everyone realizes they have a lot more stuff than they realize! It is also very hard on the nerves and very exhausting. It was just as hard on our pets.

I had to get Buster and Maggie ready too. Maggie

was a very small kitty so I wanted to get her vaccines before we left. I wanted to have them done a few days apart because of her small size. I took her to the vet in Las Vegas and asked them to give her the first set but to watch her to see how she reacts, and I will pick her up when she's ready.

I dropped her off early in the morning the next day. I figured it would be a couple of days but they called me the next morning and said she was ready. We decided to go ahead and move that day too. I went to get her and she seemed okay. They said it all went well and that she would be alright. But as we were driving, she started panting a lot and I thought maybe she was having an anxiety attack. I was so scared by the time we got to Parker, where we had to stay in our trailer a few days before our house would be ready. I should have taken her immediately to a local vet.

I have the reputation of being a worrywart so Ted thought we should settle her in and let her rest until the next day. So, I waited. I made her bed in our room and watched her all day. She would not eat and was not drinking. Ted told me not to worry and that she would be fine. But I couldn't get to sleep and kept getting up to check on her. I finally fell asleep in the early hours but when Ted woke me up, he said I think you were right. Maggie is not looking good. This was over the Easter holiday weekend, and I had to call a vet for an emergency visit.

I was so glad I did. Maggie was so dehydrated from the shots we almost lost her. Now anytime I feel my pets are in trouble, I call. Yeah, I know I'm a worrywart. But I'm okay with that even if I also know I sometimes drive my veterinarian and my husband a little CRAZY!!!

When Maggie got better and the house was ready, we moved into our new home. It was so strange and exciting at the same time. But having my little family and God with me I knew we were going to be okay to begin our next chapter in our life together. I'm glad I didn't stay stuck in my safe little world because then I never would have found my Turbo.

Meeting Turbo

We had been in Havasu for about three years and everything was going fine. We weren't having to go into Vegas anymore to supplement our work, business was picking up. We were working a lot, so Buster was being left alone much more. I felt bad for leaving him alone, so I was thinking about getting another dog, but never got around to looking for one at the animal shelter. I was dropping Buster off one day to the groomers and there was this adorable cute dog there. He looked like a terrier mix and he kept looking at me while she was grooming him and he looked like he was smiling at me. I don't know what came over me to ask, but I said if he ever needs a home please let me know. He reminded me of the Bandit I had lost. Maybe this was a second chance to do right by him.

Well, 'funny you asked' she said. The owner was having second thoughts about keeping him. They had lost their family dog very recently and were now aware that maybe they had adopted another one too soon after its death. They loved him but wanted what was best for him. I said that's okay, if it's meant to happen it will be. I took Buster home and didn't hear about the little smiling dog for a long time. Then one day I got a call from my groomer and she said, 'remember that cute dog that you liked?' I said yes. Well his owner had finally decided they were not going to keep him. They were going to take him to the animal shelter. I got their phone number and called the owner and asked her if we could see him. That's where it all begins.

It had been a while since I had seen him and I admit I kept thinking; do I really want another dog? Do I have time? Because when we take a pet, we take them for life. Just because things get crazy and hard, we don't get rid of them. I told her I needed to talk to Ted and I would let her know by the end of the day. Of course, Ted said it was up to me. I could not forget that wonderful cute face, so that was that. When we finally called the owner, it was crazy that they only lived around the block from us. We set up a time to come by to see him that week. I was hoping this was the right thing to do but his little face and that smile kept stealing into my heart.

We pulled up to the house and I was very nervous. What if this dog didn't like Ted or I. I guess we will find out soon enough. We rang the doorbell, but I didn't hear any barking. That's good, he's well behaved. The owner came to the door and when I looked at her face, she looked sad but relieved at the same time. I understood how she must feel, because I had to find a pet a new home once and you hope someone will love and take care of them. The guilt of letting a pet go is something I still live with today.

We sat down on the couch looking for the smiling face. She said he was outside in the pool. He loved the pool. She couldn't keep him out of it. I could see Teds face light up. A water dog! Hey, wait just a darn minute...he is supposed to be for me. To keep me company! She opened the sliding glass door and he came dripping up to me with that smile. The cute smile I remembered from the very first time I saw him. I knew I wanted him right then, no more wondering at all. Do you believe you can love a person or an animal at first sight? I do. Because I knew I loved this little guy from the first time I had seen that smile. We are going to be best friends forever. Yep, there was no question in my mind... this was love at first sight!

On the way home, as I'm sitting there holding this little bundle of wet cuteness in my lap, he reminded me a little of my other dog Bandit. This made me a little sad but it also made me very determined. I knew no matter what… I would do whatever it takes to give him and all my other pets a wonderful life.

The one thing Ted and I both agreed on was that we were going to change his name. He did not look like a Tinker to us and he had way more energy than someone tinkering around. He was on turbo-boost. He was turbo-charged like a turbo-engine. Sure, Turbo! It fit his character and boosted his image.

Then my thoughts turned in another direction. What about Buster and Maggie? Would this upset them so much that they would start acting up? Well it's a little late now to be thinking about them! I had taken this guy for life and will have to see how this goes.

We let Turbo meet Maggie first. She liked him so she did her kitty thing and rubbed up against him. It took him a second to realize she was not a dog. But he was always up for some playtime. As he began sniffing her and bumping into her to make her run so he could chase her, she just sat there. Oh, she let him get close, real close. When he got too close, she swatted him across the face. He froze and started barking at her. She looked at him and walked away.

We had decided to put Buster in the back yard so he and Turbo could get their first look of each other with the safety of the sliding glass door between them. This was how I had met Buster myself!

I admit I was nervous for the Turbo. Ted went outside and put a leash on Buster. I stayed inside and put one on Turbo. But when I looked through the glass, Buster looked like Wyatt Earp in a re-creation of the gunfight at the Okay Corral. He was standing stiff, feet spread apart, at one end of the corral and Turbo was at the other end. There was no barking. Buster was staring him down. This was a standoff. Maggie just sat back watching them. She was waiting to see who would come out of this fight alive.

Then Ted slid the glass door open. My heart was pounding. I was waiting to see what would happen. And then NOTHING!! Buster came inside to sniff Turbo, turned around, and just walked off. He had been hanging around Maggie way too long. He was too old for this much energy.

Turbo was going crazy, he wanted to play. Surely Buster would play with him? When we let Turbo off the leash he went up to Buster and did the happy dog dance around him. Buster had to let this guy know he was the king of this house and Turbo was the jester!! His low growl convinced Turbo of the pecking order.

From then on, they were best friends. Even though Turbo was an open book and showed how much he loved Buster… Buster always played hard-to-get. He was a tough guy, Mr. Aloof, Mr. Independent. Except when Turbo was not around… If Turbo was at a doctor visit or with Ted at the lake… I would catch Buster watching the door till Turbo got home. Yeah, then he was Mr. Anxious, Mr. Lonely Heart, Mr. Where is My Buddy. As soon as Turbo appeared again, the act was back on. Buster didn't fool anyone, not even Turbo.

Through the years Turbo helped Buster learn new things. How to use the doggie dog was an example. To Buster, the doggie door was like a child being afraid of the boogey-man. The look of fear on his face was a sight to see. I felt so bad that he was so afraid to go through that door. But not Turbo, he would go through it at Mach speed. No worries about it for him.

One day we were watching TV and Turbo went through the doggie door and came right back in and went up to Buster and barked. He took off again, ran through the door, came back again, and barked. He did this several times and we watched as Buster got closer and closer to the doggie door each time Turbo would come in and bark. After several more times, when Buster got right at the opening, Turbo went behind Buster and barked several times. We were never sure if Turbo *scared* Buster through that door or if he gave him the courage to try. Whatever, it worked.

It took a couple of tries for Buster to realize he could do the same thing and get himself back through that door to the inside. You would have thought Turbo had won the lottery!! He pranced around like he was so proud of himself. I know we were proud of him. We were proud of Buster too. I think after that he let Turbo follow him around with a better attitude. He let him get a little closer when they slept… well, at least at paws length.

Buster never got into trouble; he was very easy going most of the time. It was Turbo who we had to keep an eye on. He liked to be the center of attention. I remember not too long after getting Turbo, there was an issue with a bottle of black ink. This particular day I guess he felt like no one was paying any attention to him. I saw him go down the hall to the office/bedroom and then he came running out like he had a coyote hot on his tail. We thought the turbo-streak was cute until we saw a black bottle hanging from his mouth.

He must have been up on the desk but we knew that black bottle meant serious trouble! We both got up to chase him. Boy, was that a mistake. He thought it was play time and ran behind the couch. Well you know what happened… it was on the carpet, the wall behind the couch and all over him!! Once we finally caught him and looked at the mess, we started laughing. Turbo was too darn smart for his own good and we have the memories and stains to prove it. The couch had to stay where it was.

The Terrible Two's
{Ted and Turbo}

Now Buster and Turbo were buds, but who would have thought that Ted and Turbo would have become the best of friends. He was supposed to be my dog. When he was feeling sick or feeling down it was me, he would come to. But when it was play time it was all Ted. They told us that Turbo liked the pool, but that was nothing compared to the lake. The first time Ted pulled out the boat Turbo was looking out the window and watching him like a hawk.

When he realized he was going to go, that was another story!! We took both dogs a few times but Buster was like me, not into it so much. I work out in the heat all day so I really didn't want to be out in it on my days off. The cooler weather was a lot nicer, so Ted would take Turbo every time he went unless it was way too hot out. And if Ted didn't take him, he would have to hook up the boat the night before and close the door so Turbo could not hear or see what was going on! I don't know how Turbo knew, but Ted could walk out in his swim trunks and tee shirt and Turbo would still know he was going out on the lake.

Turbo loved it! He would lay on the boogie boards

and float around with Ted, he even went tubing with him. I was not to happy about that until I saw the photos. Turbo looked like he was having a ball. I think Ted was getting a complex. Every time he talked to people; they would say 'hi Turbo what's up'… not hi Ted what's up! And when Turbo was not able to go, they wouldn't say hi Ted, *nooo* it was 'where's Turbo?'

But Ted didn't really care. That was his buddy and his friend. To have him for the lake was great. But when we found out he loved Glamis' sand dunes!! Oh boy! Ted was in heaven. I remember our first trip with Turbo and Buster, we were setting up camp and we hand our quads for each of us, they were sitting out on the sand and I noticed I could not see Turbo. He was on a lead rope so he could walk around, and I looked out and there he was just sitting on my quad like… okay hurry up let's go for a ride! I couldn't believe it. When Ted saw him sitting there waiting, he said now I have someone to go with me if you don't want to come. I'm glad because I quit going and it became the boys weekend trips! Which was okay with me. I had the whole weekend at home to do what I wanted to do, and I had Buster and Maggie with me.

My mother was visiting when Ted decided to go to Glamis. My mom and I planned to do some shopping in Yuma. On the way down to Yuma we were following Ted and Turbo in the motor home when we heard cars starting to honk and looked around to see what the problem could be. Well, it was not road rage. No, it was Turbo. You have to remember he is a dog. As much as we thought of him as a people… he was a dog. Turbo was in the back window of the motor home with a pillow he had found and was in love with. He was putting on quite a show for the passing motorists and they were laughing and honking to encourage him. I was not laughing I was on the phone to tell Ted to pull over!

Ted was a little confused at the commotion and when I told him what HIS dog was doing… he started laughing but he did pull over. It was quite a struggle to get Turbo's friend away from him and I was never so glad to hear my mother laugh in my life. When I talked to my mother about writing about Turbo, she reminded me I should be sure and tell this story because after all, he was a dog and he could always make us laugh.

Dealing With Loss

Do animals mourn like people at the loss of their companions? I believe with all my heart they do. I have never seen it before, but the day we lost our Buster, the way that Turbo handled it was proof it was true. It was so true, and heart wrenching. Things were going good for us, and Buster, Turbo and Maggie accepted each other. Buster always let Turbo hang around him at a distance. I hoped he would be closer to Turbo because Turbo was a dog who loved to be anywhere you were. But he took whatever attention he got from Buster. We thought things were going well in our lives and the dogs and cat were all happy and healthy. But we were about to find out not everyone was healthy.

I noticed a few days before he had a grooming appointment that Buster didn't have much of an appetite. He ate a little bit, went to the bathroom, and was drinking okay. But I kept my eye on him to make sure there was no blood in the stool. The day I was taking him to the groomers, he had a very runny stool that didn't look too good. But he seemed okay. It's so hard to tell because they hide their pain so well, I wish they could talk. When I dropped him off at the groomers, I asked them to keep an eye on him and if he acts different to call me right away. I told them about his stool and that he may not be feeling well. When I called to see if he was ready, they said he did okay, but he peed in the kennel. He had never done that before. They felt he was not his normal self either. I called the vet and took him right in.

The vet did his exam and said they would like to keep him to get ex rays and blood work. When they went to take him back, I stopped him so I could hug him. As they started to take him back, I got such a sad feeling in my heart that I would never see him again. That was the last time I saw Buster's adoring eyes on me. It was with a very sad heart that we lost Buster Brown Chesher that night. On June 3rd 2006 Buster was cremated and we kept his ashes.

I knew Turbo knew something was wrong. Ted knew Turbo knew something was wrong. Because Turbo knew something was wrong! The day Buster did not come home, Turbo sat by the back door and waited. When Buster still did not show up, he would pace from the office down the hall to the back door.

I had to not cry when Turbo was around because he could sense something from my reactions. To see him pace and look like panic was in his eyes was just heart wrenching. But we had to carry on just like every other day before Buster died. We had to leave Turbo alone at home. And each day, when we came home, we had to wonder about what Turbo had been up to.

He was acting out, letting us know he was sad too.

One day we came home and he pulled, or should I say he tried to pull, a large area rug out the doggie door. He pulled the queen bed skirt off the bed one day. He ripped up pillows from the couch. But the hardest thing to deal with was when he would lay where Buster used to lay and still look for him at the back door.

This had gone on for a couple of months but I didn't want to get another dog to keep him company. I was so glad my friend, who lived across the street, came up with a great idea for Turbo to come over when we were gone and play with her dogs. We did that until he became over protective of her and he would not let her dogs around her.

Ted said maybe it was time to find another dog for Turbo. It had been over a year now since Buster passed. We started going to visit our local animal shelter but we could never agree on a dog. I finally told Ted if God wants us to have another dog, he will put the right one in our lives, when we are ready.

Rachel

Wouldn't you know it… one day, shortly after we had made the decision to wait for the right pet, we were cleaning windows at a grooming facility. The groomer was talking on the phone to someone about a dog she had groomed for years. We understood from the conversation that the owner didn't want her anymore and was trying to get rid of her.

When she got off the phone, she told us about Rachel. She was a cock-a-poo, Poodle mixed with Cocker Spaniel. Ted and I looked at each other and asked her where was this dog? Wouldn't you know… she just happened to be at our vet's office. For some reason we both wanted to see her. We thought she would be a small dog for Turbo. But when got there and they brought her in, her head was down and she looked so sad. She wasn't small like Turbo; she was about Busters size. They told us to think about it, but before I could say anything Ted said we will take her.

I just looked at him and thought this was meant to be. God put us in the exact place to meet Rachel and we both wanted her so it was meant to be. I remember asking God that when it's the right dog to please let us know. And he did.

The vet told us all they knew about her. They said she mostly lived on the small porch of the owner's condo. They also thought the owners were very hard on her because of how Rachel reacts to things. The vet had been told she bit the groomer but we knew that wasn't true because we knew her groomer. We were sure they just didn't what her anymore. And that was okay because she is a blessing to us. We did find out later that she didn't like her paws touched and you better stay away from her food. Yes, she will bite if you try to get between her and food. That is not all that uncommon for animals so we learned to adjust to her and she learned to adjust to us. It's called respect.

We hoped she would be best friends with Turbo, but she was not. Oh no… she was a female version of our aloof Buster. So be careful what you pray for. I missed Buster so much and who he was, that God did answer my prayers by giving us another Buster… only the gender was different. Maggie definitely accepted Rachel as Busters replacement and I think Turbo took to her so easily because she was so much like Buster! The hierarchy was intact and they all got along. Turbo seemed so much happier and so were we. I am glad it all worked out.

What? Diabetic

As I look back, I can clearly see we were brought to Lake Havasu City, Arizona for a reason. I see God was always taking care of us. We made it through some very hard times but we have been blessed with very wonderful clients who stayed loyal to us through it all and still do to this day. I have learned that when we listen to God and slow down a bit, which I have to say I'm still working on both, then we find He is in control. My love for God and Jesus is strong, but I'm human and I may have to hear it more than once!

When Turbo started having some health issues, I was not prepared for what was going to happen next. You know how much Turbo loved going to Glamis and being anywhere we were? On one trip I noticed he was tired a lot and didn't have much energy. And he was drinking so much water! I thought he was just hot being out on the sand. But when we got home, he still wanted to go outside and pee all the time. For the next two days I was sleeping on the couch because he was up so often. He wanted to go outside all night. In the morning I called and made an appointment to see the vet. They let me bring him in the next day.

He usually liked our car rides but he seemed so nervous and all over the place. I knew something was wrong. I had to leave him for the day so they could run some tests and they would call me when they had the results. They called me later that day and said for us to come in and get Turbo, and they would go over the results.

I was so nervous waiting in the room and then the door opened and the vet came in and said your little guy is a diabetic. This was in June of 2010.

That explains his fast weight loss from 22 pounds to 16 pounds. His hair was so full and pretty that I didn't know he had lost so much weight.

We went to pick him up and they explained the diet change he would need and how to give him his shots. WHAT SHOTS!! I thought I could give him pills. No shots. I'm trying to wrap my head around him being diabetic let alone me having to put a needle in his neck. Not once, but twice a day. I asked if this was common in his breed? He was a Yorkie but I believe he may have been a mix. He was bigger and his hair was not long. But we loved him no matter what. They said yes, a lot has to do with the breed and diet.

I felt so bad. I thought I was doing everything right for him, and I felt it was my fault he got this disease. But no matter what, I will do whatever I need to do for him or any of my pets. *Sooo*, I began the new diet and the shots.

Here I go, the first shot. I put my big girl panties on and I gathered his skin from his neck and went to insert the needle and he moved and screamed. Oh no! I put it in too far or I hit the wrong spot. Crappers. All I could do was go in the kitchen and cry. Then I called the vet and they said I can't act like I don't know what I'm doing and if I miss then try again. Act? There was no acting involved. I didn't know what I was doing. They told me he can tell that I'm upset and he will play to my emotions. Oh really, like I don't know he has had my number from the start? Maybe I could be tricky?

I got him a treat. When he went to eat it… I slipped that shot right in! And what do you know? I really did it and it wasn't so hard after all!! Once I figured it out, it was so much easier than I thought. And I had to remind myself that I was helping to give him a longer and better quality of life.

The downside of insulin is that I was told he would lose his sight. Usually within three to four months from starting a dog on insulin. We had to prepare for that. We made sure we liked how all the furniture, tables and stationary items were placed in our house and knew we could never move them again. People learn their surroundings and so do animals so by the time we thought he wouldn't be able to see; he would know his way around enough he would not bump into things.

Turbo was using an insulin for dogs. It took several tries to get his blood sugar levels right. Unlike humans,

Turbo did not have test strips to monitor his sugar levels several times a day and adjust his shots accordingly. I had to observe his behavior for any changes. Was he drinking excessive amounts of water? Was he having to go outside to pee all the time? Was he listless or a little confused? If I saw that these things were increasing, I called the vet and they would do a blood series to see if the insulin needed to be adjusted. It was very trial and error.

But just when we seemed to get him level, the company who supplies the insulin for animals wanted to discontinue the product. Are you kidding me??? We just got him stable! Now they were going to create a whole new set of issues! Would the dosage change? Would that cause damage to his kidneys, his heart, his eyes, his quality of life? Would a new insulin make it better or worse for Turbo?

It turned out this new product was for the better. They put Turbo on human insulin. It took a while to adjust it, but in the end, it worked so much better for him. And I was able to purchase the human insulin and the syringes at a lower price at Walmart. With Turbo's levels more stable, we also had fewer visits to the vet for blood sugar tests.

With all of the diabetic changes going on in Turbo's body, we tried to keep things as normal as possible. I found that when I took Turbo for a walk now, it had to be shorter distances and I almost always had to pick him up to carry him on the way home. He began favoring his foot a little but one day he was definitely limping. We thought he jumped off the couch and sprained his leg. The vet looked at it and did an x-ray but there were no breaks and he could still walk on it. They told us to keep an eye on it.

We thought things were going okay, he didn't have me up as much during the night. That was a relief because sometimes I tried to sleep on the couch so I would not wake Ted up. The couch was closer to the back door for me to let Turbo in and out all night when his levels were not stable.

But a week went by and Turbo did not want to use his leg. He was holding it up and not putting any weight on it. That did not slow him down, he would run and do everything the same. I made another appointment for the vet to check on his leg. They took another x-ray and noticed there was a foggy mass around his bone. All I could think of was, is this cancer?

The vet wanted to run a Valley Fever test. He wanted to see if it may be that, or if not, rule it out. We waited for the results to get back which took about a week. Then I got a call, it was Valley Fever. Again… are you kidding me????? One more thing for him to bear. Was I doing the right thing? Was he going to be in pain? We talked about it and as long as he was happy and eating and pooping, we had to keep trying.

Unless you live in the southwest you've probably

never heard of Valley Fever. It is an endo-spore found in the desert soil of New Mexico, Southwestern Texas, Southwestern Californian deserts, and Arizona. Since it is a fungus that grows in the soil, dogs typically get it from digging in the dirt, sniffing around holes in the desert or from the humongous dust storms we get on occasion. People and other animals get Valley Fever too but it is not contagious. Since it is airborne it affects the lungs with symptoms like a harsh dry cough, a fever, a lack of appetite, and lethargy. When the infection spreads outside the lungs it commonly causes lameness by affecting the bones. It can occur in almost any organ but for Turbo, it was his leg.

The medication for this disease was a pill he had to take twice a day but I could hide it in a treat so at least it wasn't difficult to get him to take it. But the new medicine had side effects that masked the diabetic behaviors that I used to monitor his insulin. It made him drink more water and again, pee all the time. To say it was difficult to keep tabs on his sugar levels with this new setback, is an understatement. At least the medicine helped the bones in his legs enough that he quit limping but now our walks had to be limited. We only walked him up and down our block as his stamina was so limited.

There were still nights when I didn't get any sleep but there were fewer of them. Maggie had a scare of not eating but I prayed to God to help her and Turbo and she was fine in a few days. Turbo was outside one day and I always went outside with the dogs because of our coyote problem. Even with an eight-foot fence the coyotes can climb over and get their next meal. I looked around and I didn't see Turbo so I walked around the corner of the house and he was just standing there. I called for him but he would not move. I walked up to him and he flinched. I looked at his eyes and I knew he was blind. They were right. It was about three and a half months from him starting on the insulin until he lost his sight.

I got Ted and we both cried. I think it was harder on us than it was for Turbo. Let me tell you one thing, through all the shots and pills and diet changes and losing his sight, I know in my heart that he handled it so much better than I would have. He still tried to always be around us and love us, even when he felt so bad. He was my HERO!!!

Turbo still sweet, even blind.

Ben the Blessing

What can I say about Ben? He is a ten-pound Maltese who thinks he's a Great Dane and sometimes has the attitude to go with it. But he was a blessing from God from the moment we brought him home. He was Turbo's life saver, and I literally mean his life. It was almost like he gave Turbo another reason to live. Turbo loved us so much, but his connection with Ben was what brought him back to us.

Even though Turbo had his independent Rachel around, Turbo seemed so sad and blue. I felt so bad for him because he could not go with Ted to Glamis or on the lake. Ted tried to take Turbo to the lake with him a few times but Turbo could not see and he had so little energy. He seemed so lost.

Before his illness if Ted had on swimming trunks Turbo would run in excited circles. If he heard the garage door open, he knew the boat was not far behind. But Ted was torn in two every time he left to go to the lake now without his buddy. He would look back and see Turbo sightlessly looking out the window knowing he had heard the garage door but not able to see Ted or the boat he loved. We knew how much he missed the water, he loved to swim so much, so we decided to get an above-ground pool. Once again, he could go swimming with Ted. He loved that. But his overall sadness did not seem to get any better.

One day I had to go to the vet's office and when I walked in the door the vet's wife was holding this cute small white dog. I'm not sure why really, but I asked her what was going on and she said the owners just dropped him off. They were an older couple and the little dog had darted between his legs and he tripped and fell. It was hours before the gentleman was found in their backyard so they thought it was best to find the dog a new home. They were very upset about this but the risk of another accident was too critical to the gentleman's health.

I don't know what I was thinking but I said if he needs a home call me. What? What did I just say? What was I thinking? I was thinking of Turbo, so I would like you to meet Ben.

I was so nervous about bringing Ben home. Will it change Rachel or Turbos attitude? Well, there was no turning back now. When I take a pet, I take them for life, so here goes. It reminded me of when you were new in school and you walked to your desk and all eyes were on you. That's what it looked like when I brought Ben into the house and let them smell each other on either side of a baby gate for safety's sake.

Even though Turbo couldn't see, you would have never guessed it. His head was in the air sniffing like crazy. Rachel took one whiff of Ben and lost interest. She left Turbo to deal with this guy. It was all Turbo and Ben. After a few minutes I opened the gate and Ben stood still and at attention. He let Turbo smell him and then it was his turn.

It was quite amusing to watch them go in circles smelling each other's butts, but that's their hello. Could you picture people doing that? I'm sure that would not go so well! But all-in-all this meeting was a success so our lives changed again, lol! It was much better having Ben in our lives.

Turbo had his favorite spot next to me in the big chair I sat in, so Ben sat on my other side. Rachel liked to be on the ottoman close by and of course Maggie had first dibs on my lap. It may seem like I favored Turbo, but I loved them all the same, in different ways. I wanted to keep peace so I always made sure they kept their same spots so the pecking order was not violated. Oh, sometimes Ben wanted to take Turbos place in the chair but I didn't let that happen. Ben was younger and he could have taken advantage of the little blind man but I wanted the pack's code to stay intact. And it worked out.

Sometimes I felt sorry for Ben, the new-comer. I hope he knew it was to keep order. That didn't stop some fighting at times over food. Ben and Rachel both love their food and do not want to share. I started feeding them in different places in the house. Rachel had her buffet in our bedroom, Turbo had his in the bathroom, and Ben had his in the kitchen. They all liked having their own space to eat in peace. I am sure it helped Ben merge into our household so easily.

A Mixture of Problems

I had quite a few scares with Turbo. The month of May, 2013, was by far the hardest for me. He started acting strange. He would stand in one spot and it was like he had forgotten where he was. He started going outside a lot again, three to four times a night. I had his sugar count for his insulin checked and it was okay so I was at a loss. He was not wanting to eat and I had to tell myself not to be selfish and think with my head and not with my heart. Yeah right. It finally came to the prospect of deciding if I was going to have to make a hard decision. A decision I did not want to make. But was Turbo's quality of life still good? I am a wimp but I am not a quitter so I made a deal with myself. If he was not better by the next day, which was Sunday, then Ted and I would have to talk.

That night was the worst one yet. I laid out on the back porch with him, with my flash light, to make sure he was breathing and I prayed to God that if I could not give him the life he deserved, please take him. He had been a loyal and wonderful dog and he deserved a better way to leave this earth. I got up in the morning and Ted had let Ben out. He ran over to Turbo and would not leave him. I had to go inside; I could not stop crying. You see Ben always treated Turbo like a dog without any issues and he would tussle with him wanting a play pal. But when Turbo was sick… Ben would protect him. I had to get it together and feed Ben, Rachel and Maggie but I really didn't think Turbo would eat. I kept praying and whatever your beliefs are… I truly believe in prayer.

Turbo came over and wanted something to eat. WHAT? Is that possible after two days? I gave him a little bit and later I gave him some more. He kept it down and I have never been happier to see him poop than that day!!!!

Things were staying steady, until we had another blood test to check his sugar levels and wouldn't you know, another issue… his thyroid. I wish I could talk to my pets, so I knew what to do for them, but that's why we have veterinarians to help us with our decisions. They told us Turbo was not producing enough thyroid. And, of course, they had to put him on medication to help him with that.

I remember someone telling me they would not do what I am doing for Turbo. That they would not change their whole life for them. But it's what I do, it's what I had to do. It was never a burden for me. It was an honor. And he was so inspiring to me to see him never give up.

We were in the month of September. Our anniversary was coming up. It was our sixteenth year.

And as I thought about my life, I realized how fast every day was passing and I admit it was a little scary. You know how people say if only they knew then what they know now… they would do things different? Well I thought of that too, and honestly, I would do a few things different in my life, but then I took a minute to sit back and I realized that any changes in my life before, wouldn't have me where I am today.

For one thing, I would never have met Ted or known the wonderful journey which led us to Lake Havasu. I wouldn't have my home or have known the blessings in my life with our business and friends here. And when I looked at my pets, I never would have met Buster or had my beautiful Maggie, Rachel, Ben and of course Turbo. To think they never would have been in my life, is something that makes my heart sad.

We can say 'if only' till the cows come home.

I could have… if only I had…

But then that would mean the people and choices which have made me stronger and more complete would never have been in my life. I admit it has not always been easy. In my weaker moments I feel the first part of my life was something I wasted. But if I hadn't gone through the bad, I would not have appreciated the wonder of the good. I now know I would never want to change a thing.

Turbo and Ben's friendship was great, but when Turbo really started having more bad days it was hard for me to watch. Watching how Ben reacted to Turbo was even harder. When Turbo would go and lay out on the stone walkway and not want to move, Ben would go over and smell him, and just lay down next to him. Ben would never try to provoke him; it was like he knew he was not well and just stayed by his side. But the moment Turbo felt better, well *then,* all bets were off!!

I could see the better days were getting fewer and further between. I was getting up four times a night to get Turbo off the bed and put him in the bathroom where the floor was cooler, and then I would hear him come down the hall and I got up to put him back on the bed. You would think that Ben would try to take his spot on the bed while he was gone, but he never did. When I put Turbo back on the bed, they would settle in to their normal places.

Of course, animals claim their personal territory. Maggie slept around my neck or under my arm. But Rachel oddly enough always opted to sleep alone. With the high hundred plus temperatures we have in this desert community she chose to sleep on our cool bathroom floor next to the air conditioning vent. She stayed cool and slept undisturbed. Smart huh? But I often thought she secretly wanted to be on the bed with us, if it wasn't so crowded. So, would you believe… we actually upgraded to a king-sized bed. Yep, just to accommodate our pets!!

But still Rachel would come up, do a circle dance and jump down to go back to her personal exile. Then I got the bright idea to put an ottoman at the end of the bed, to extend it even more. And what do you know? Rachel claimed it… she actually thought this was her own personal throne. None of the others bothered her or tried to share it so now she slept near us but didn't have to worry about getting kicked or squashed like the rest of us. Having a jam-packed pet bed has never bothered me. At least I always knew where everyone was. But I am thankful Ted didn't mind it either.

We kept an eye on Turbo's health with regular visits to the veterinarian's office which now felt like his second home. I thank God for all their help.

We were so happy to have another thanksgiving with all the dogs and Maggie. We used to walk them a lot but with Turbo's health, he had a really hard time walking and it seemed harder for him to breathe, so we limited the walking and did a lot more back yard activities.

Now Rachel was getting older too, and we noticed she seemed tired and breathing harder when we were walking her, so she went to the veterinarian's office and we had to put her on medication that would help her heart. It seemed to work. I thanked God because it would really be sad to have two very sick dogs at the same time.

Even at Christmas Turbo was still here to help us celebrate! He was still having me get up and down a lot at night and I always worried about him being in pain. But I discussed this with our veterinarian. They gave me the signs to look for and he may have had a few moments where we wondered, but he would turn around and be his happy self again.

Ben's health was good. He had times where the nerves in his neck, from jumping around so much, would bother him but all in all everyone was doing well. Ted and I were so busy with work and I didn't mind staying home with the pets. I always felt bad that Turbo could not go with Ted to Glamis or on the boat anymore. You really had to keep an eye on him more with him being blind, and if he got sick, he was so far away in Glamis that we didn't want to chance it.

Ted tried several times to take Turbo to the lake with him. Turbo liked to hear the other boaters talk to him, listen to the duck's quack and sniff the fishy air. But after a couple of hours Ted had to call me to come and get Turbo because he had run out of energy. It is so true, either animal or human, enjoy your life now because you never know when it can change. Never take your health for granted. Love hard, be happy, live fully and be thankful to God every day for everything.

I was glad we all got through 2013 and things were going well so far in 2014. We tried to keep things just like always with Turbo. Occasionally we would still walk all of them together and when people saw our little parade, they would comment on how cute they looked. They almost always noticed Turbo was in the lead with Ben and Rachel submissively following him. But when they found out that Turbo was blind, it was funny to see the look on their face.

We did notice that sometimes when Turbo would be eating or just outside walking his back leg would give out. As soon as it did, he would get right back up and go on like always. But we started keeping track on how often this happened so if it got too frequent, we could get him back to the vet's office.

We talked about this and if we were keeping him around for us and not thinking about him. But I asked God to help me know when it was time and not let him suffer. He was on diabetic insulin, Valley Fever and the thyroid medication and would be for his lifetime. But it was monitored to make sure he was okay. The Vet agreed that as long as he's eating and drinking and everything was fine, let him be his happy self.

One day I remember leaving the vacuum out in the middle of the living room and went to get some water. I was so good at not changing things around in the house but I heard a loud thump. I knew that thump meant Turbo had run into the vacuum. Evidently, he had hit it pretty hard too for me to hear it in another room. I went in and checked on him to make sure he was okay but had to quickly go back to the kitchen. I was laughing and crying at the same time.

It's now June 2014, and summer is not my favorite time of the year in this desert. I sincerely doubt if it is anyone's favorite time after it hits one hundred and twenty degrees during the day with night time temps only slightly lower. I try to tell myself that if I did not work outside in it, maybe I would feel a little differently about it. But I doubt it. It can be 95 degrees by 8:00am and get up to 120 or more by noon. I admit that I complain about the heat, but I have been trying to do better about that. {NOT}!!

If its hard on me I know it's hard on all the pets. Visitors may not know this but by May or June it can be too hot to walk your pets. I get so upset when I see people leave their dogs in a hot car or let them walk on the hot cement or blacktop. They should take their shoes off and try to walk on it or sit in a hot car with the windows rolled up. Common sense tells you that you shouldn't do that to a child or to a pet in this extreme heat.

With not being able to walk the dogs in this heat and with Turbo not being able to go with Ted to the lake anymore, we got an above ground pool. I say it was for Ted mostly but I really think we both wanted it for Turbo. Rachel did not like the water. Ben was okay with swimming but he was not a big fan like Turbo. Also, Ben is a white-haired dog with very pink skin and he easily got sunburned even after only a short time outside. Ted would take a small knee board and push them around on it. Turbo got a lot of exercise while swimming and floating around with Ted but mostly he loved, loved, loved the water.

July was very hot and this year it was really muggy. It feels like I'm always sweating. I was happy to see that all the pets were doing well, but I started noticing Turbo did not want to eat as much as he had been. There were times if he didn't get a certain food he would not eat. I understand that getting the same food over and over would get very boring. Because his diet was so strict, I did feel sorry for him.

But it went on for three days so I looked in his mouth. It seemed he may have lost another tooth, and one of his other teeth seemed to be disintegrated. I would forget that Turbo was thirteen years old and this could be as a result of old age. I tried to keep them clean and fortunately he would let me brush his teeth. But he needed a cleaning and possible extractions. I was so worried about him being under an anesthetic with all his health issues. But if he has bad teeth and an infection, that's not good for him either.

While Turbo was getting his teeth done, I was busy worrying thinking what if he doesn't come home? I was trying to prepare myself for losing Turbo but not having much success. I was so worried all day all I could do was pray. GREAT NEWS!!!! He came through it like a champ. He seemed to feel so much better and was full of energy again. I didn't even realize I had tears running down my face, until Ted told me. But when I looked at him, which he would not admit, his eyes were full of tears too.

Every day was a blessing to have all my pets. We had made it through another year, another Christmas and another New Year's together. I can't explain it but I felt even though we had survived this last year, there was probably very little time left for Turbo. Because of Turbos health I had refused to travel away from home because of what might happen when we were gone. These pets are my family and I hated to think about their dying or getting sick while we were traveling. Where would we find a Vet? And of course, leaving them at home, even with a pet-sitter was out of the question. What if one of them were to die while we were gone? They would be alone, without Ted or I and that was something I didn't think I could live with. But it was evident we both needed some time away from work and I wanted to get away with Ted and my fur babies.

We hadn't been to the ocean in such a long time, which is my happy place, so we decided to load up the motor home and head to Huntington Beach California. We made a wood bench to fit in between the console of the motor home so Ben and Turbo could be next to each other. Sometimes, well most of the time, Ben sat in my lap and Turbo between Ted and I, because most of the time he could not make up his mind who to sit next too.

Rachel sat on the floor but would put her head on the top of the bench and sit there and fall asleep. It didn't matter to her that she just had a tiny corner of the bench as long as she was near me, and she could see what was going on. It was a lot of work with three dogs, right? Yes, it was just like having small kids. Only we had to make sure ours were all on a leash for walks, that they all had separate spots for eating, and that we gave them the same amount of attention. Okay, so I always felt a little guilty about giving so much more time to Turbo, giving him his shots and medications. But I know Rachel and Ben both knew that it was what had to be done. We were all ready and settled in so away we went!! California here we come!!

I could not wait to smell the beautiful ocean air and put my feet in the sand and water. If it were ever able to have a small little place by the ocean, that would be on my list!! But just being able to go and visit I will take whenever I can. As we were getting closer, I could smell the ocean in the air and Ted looked over at me and laughed. I asked what was so funny and he said I looked like the dogs when they are smelling the air.

I took that as a compliment. I looked at them and Turbo and Ben were putting their nose out the window and smelling the air. What can I say, they got that from me!!! We got to the RV park and got things settled in and I could not wait to get out and see everything. So, we walked all the dogs, they had a nice grassy area for them and when we took them back, they were all exhausted and crashed for a nap.

We had set up an area around the couch so if Turbo tried to jump down, he would not hurt his leg. Because of his blindness, just like at home, everything had to be Turbo proof.

We had decided on this trip not to pull a car as it was too much of a hassle to find a trailer that would tow my car and we didn't want to buy a trailer just for this trip. We took our bikes and we rode everywhere. I saw the ocean and the beach in a way I would not have seen it by car. It was up close and personal!

When we had the critters settled in, Ted and I went on our bikes and rode to the walkway by the beach and headed north almost twelve miles to Belmont Shores. There we turned south to ride back sixteen miles to Newport Beach. To get back to Huntington Beach was almost another six miles.

There were times I was not sure I would survive all that healthy exercise, but I didn't care how tired I was or how sore I was… I was going to do it! It was beautiful weather and so much fun. It was a wonderful weekend and the dogs had fun and we all needed it.

We headed home and had two weeks of work, rest and then getting ready for the trip to Sacramento California. Now that was a long trip. But the dogs had done so great on the beach trip, no one getting car sick, loving the ride and all the new smells, that after a two-week rest, we thought we could try another trip.

The trip to Ted's parent's home in Sacramento was very long. Normally it would take around nine hours, but this time it took us almost eleven hours, because we stopped a lot so the dogs could get out and go to the bathroom and for us to stretch our legs. They were all worn out by the time we arrived and so were the non-furry fellows!

It was a very nice visit but we were told that his mom was getting the early signs of Alzheimer's. That is something no child wants to hear. But it was true. When it was time to leave, it was very early in the morning, and we tried not to wake his mom because we had said our goodbyes the night before. We were driving away and I told Ted to stop. Lia was at the front door waving so we stopped and I ran up to her and hugged her and so did Ted.

The tears came pouring out and it was very hard to leave. I'm so glad we went that weekend to see his parents because that would be the last time, we would see the Lia we had always known. I'm so glad we made the time to go. Because we really do need to take the time and remember how much we love our family, friends and loved ones. Our lives get so busy we sometimes forget to thank God, stop and breathe and appreciate what we have.

I also believe God was telling me that this may be Turbo's last trip. And it *was* the last trip for Turbo. I didn't want to believe it but he had been having more issues like getting up several times in the night and not wanting to be on the bed. I noticed Ben was watching him and not picking on him as much. It's so amazing to me how they know when something is wrong and they respect the process, better than we do.

But let me tell you something, Maggie was very upset with me for being gone and she let me know it. She went around the house all day meowing and meowing and meowing! I knew it was just temper and that she was okay because I had a friend watching her every day. I missed her too but not the attitude!

We got back in our everyday routine and all the pets seemed to settle down and were healthy except Turbo. The first week we got back was just like always, but I started noticing he didn't want to eat as much again. I thought it may be from the trip and so I just kept my eye on him. I know some will think I am over protective but pets count on you to take care of them. They can't talk or show you where they hurt, so it's up to us to be there for them just like any other person in the family. Okay, I will admit I am a little guilty of the freak-out charge but Turbo needed me.

Other than his eating habits being different, he seemed his happy-go-lucky self. Until the morning of September 30th 2014. It was a morning like any other morning. I got up, had my coffee, said my prayers, got on the computer a little bit and started getting ready for work. Once I was done, I had three dogs and a cat to take care of. I had to make sure all of their pills were taken, they all had water, they all ate, had full bellies, and went out to go for potty time before I left for work.

We start our day so early in the desert because of the heat that Ted usually leaves to begin cleaning windows before I do. After I finish all the household tasks, I would meet up with him and we would work together to finish the rest of the customers. But this day turned out to be different. Ted was finished early on a particular job so he came home to pick me up instead of me taking my car to meet him. I always like and appreciate when he picks me up and this day it also gave me a few extra minutes to finish my tasks.

All seemed fine with Turbo, he had eaten, had his shots and medication and went outside to go pee. Now that I am writing this, I believe God had Ted come home on that particular morning so I would not be alone to see Turbo take a horrible turn for the worse.

Ted went into the back room, which we turned into our office, and I was coming around the corner and there was Turbo just standing there looking at me. I looked into his eyes and it was like 'mom' somethings wrong and he went down. His back legs just gave out. I called Ted and told him what happened and he thought maybe he had another small episode from his sugar levels. But when we tried to hold him up, he could not stand at all. I was so worried about holding him, that I may hurt him, but I had to. I called the vet's office and they told me to bring him down 'asap'. I got his blanket and wrapped him in it and was ready to go.

But as I looked at Rachel and Ben, it was like they knew he may not be coming home again. They just sat there. Ben usually barks and goes in circles when I leave, but today… nothing, quiet, really quiet. Ben sat with his head down and just looked at us. Rachel lay quietly watching us too, very strange behavior for our normally bouncy dork. I was trying to keep it together and not cry because I didn't want Turbo to sense how upset I was. Ted was looking over at him and I could see the pain and sadness on his face and he reached over and touched Turbo's head. At his touch, Turbo tried to lift his head up but he couldn't.

It really is true; time seems to stop and everything takes *forever* when you are in the middle of an emergency. Especially if you want to drive as fast as possible to the vet's office. It seemed like every light was red and every driver wanted to drive like a turtle. When we *finally* reached the vet's office, I was so thankful they took us in a room right away. I didn't want people to see the tears running down my face. There were people there with new puppies and vaccinations and I was happy for them, but it was a very sad, sad day for us.

They had us leave Turbo so they could do an exam on him. But let me tell you, it was very hard to get back to work that day and try to be professional around our clients. All I could think of was Turbo being scared and I was not there to calm him down. We knew he was in good hands but it was still not easy. Anyone out there that has gone through the same thing, or close to it, will understand how we felt.

I got a call later that day from the vet's office to come back in and they would go over the results of the tests. We were just finishing up our work but for once I was dragging my feet. I had had a bad feeling all day. I didn't want to hear what they were going to tell me. But I wanted to see Turbo. I was not sure if Ted could handle this but he said that this was his buddy and I needed him there for me too.

It was time to go and hear what the doctor had to say about Turbo. I was feeling so nervous that I was sick to my stomach. They called us to come in a room and we waited for the doctor to come in. Normally you want the doctor to come in and not have to wait, but today I didn't mind waiting.

All of a sudden, I heard the door handle move and the doctor entered with a look of dread and I could feel his sadness at the same time. He started to explain the test results but I didn't take in much because everything was swirling around in my brain. Even now as I try to recall what was said, I am doing my best to relay what little information has stuck in my memory despite the sadness in my heart.

I know something was said about there being pressure on his spine from what they could see on the x-ray. The was deterioration in his bones which was causing the pressure. They gave him something to help with the swelling to see if it would ease up and bring it down. They wanted to keep him overnight to give it a chance to work and if it didn't then we needed to talk about other options. The options were very few and may not have been in Turbo's best interest due to all of his other health issues. I went back to the kennel where they kept Turbo and stayed with him for over an hour just talking to him and petting him. He was not whimpering but he was panting some and I realized he was in pain. I asked the tech about the panting and it was then I realized that even if Turbo had not looked to be in pain in the past, he had been good at masking it. It was hard to believe in all that we had done for him, he had been hurting and we hadn't seen it.

Needless to say, it was a very long night. I could not sleep. Even Ben and Rachel were restless. Ben kept looking around for Turbo, going to Turbo's hiding places and then just standing there looking at me for answers. I know they can't talk but I believe they knew something was wrong.

The next day was a work day so we had to take care of our clients but I called the vet first thing in the morning to see how Turbo was doing. They said he was quiet and sleeping now. I went to see Turbo on my way to work and he was sleeping. But they said when we can, we need to come in and discuss his situation. There was no change from last night. The medication hadn't worked and he still could not walk. It was so hard to speak but I told them I would be in after work.

I told Ted what they had said, and he was holding back tears. I couldn't stand to look at Ted's sad face so I turned my head away and continued to tell him about Turbo's condition. I asked if he was going to go with me to see him today. Ted said at this moment he wouldn't be able to. I knew how much he loved Turbo so I told him it was okay. I could handle it.

After work I went to the vet's and the doctor came in and told me that there was no change. If I wanted to take Turbo to Las Vegas to see a specialist, I could. But there was no guarantee it would help him due to his health and his age; he was thirteen years old. But he left it up to us and told us he would help us in whatever decision we made.

I asked to see him after we talked and I was not prepared to see how he looked. He was wearing a diaper because he could not hold his pee and he just looked different. How do I say this? As I'm writing this I'm crying. He looked like he was leaving me... he was dying. I could see it and my heart knew it. As I looked at him a swamping wave of guilt came over me. Seeing him this way I was sure there were times that Turbo was hurting and I didn't see it. He hid it so well but now my guilt took over. I tried to pull myself together so Turbo would not feel how sad I was. I called his name and he tried to lift his head which he could barely do. I asked them to open the kennel so I could get inside with him. I held him but I didn't want to hurt him by moving him too much. Thankfully I was told he was on pain medication. I took him in my arms and held him so tight. I stayed for a while and then I knew Ted had to come and see him because Turbo was not going to be here much longer. I knew if he didn't, he would never

90

forgive himself no matter how much it was going to hurt.

I told Turbo I would be back later and I loved him so much. I told them I would be back and I walked out to my car and opened the door, closed myself inside and bawled my eyes out. I knew what needed to be done because he was not getting any better and I didn't want him in any pain, any longer.

I knew it was going to be hard to have a conversation with Ted about what we needed to do for Turbo. I thought he didn't want to believe this was happening. Just like I didn't want to believe it. But it was happening and it had to be discussed.

I drove home and I told Ted everything that was going on with Turbo. I told him about the diaper, he was not eating, and his hair looked so bad. Ted was very upset but after we discussed what our options were, he agreed that we needed to take Turbo's pain away and let him go.

At first, he didn't think he could see Turbo like this. But I said, 'you have to, he deserves that from you. He has been your side-kick for thirteen years, and he has loved you unconditionally.' I suggested we go together and then I will leave and he can spend time with Turbo alone, as much as he needed, and then I would spend more time with him before we said our final goodbyes. He agreed but he said he could not stay there when they put him to sleep.

I understood and told him I would be there till the end. It was an honor to be in his life when he was alive and it will be an honor to be there when he draws his last breath. He won't be alone. We reach the vets office and we were taken to the back and when Ted went around the corner and saw him, well he lost it. I told him Turbo can feel you and you have to love on him without him feeling so much sadness.

Yeah right, easier said than done. He went in the kennel and pulled Turbo to his chest and Turbo looked up and licked Teds chin, and Ted hit the side of the cage and said 'why'? Ted looked at me and tears were rolling down my face. I said pull it together he's feeling how upset you are. Just love him and talk to him and call me when you are ready to leave.

I left and got a call about an hour later and headed back to the clinic. Ted looked so defeated and before he left, he asked me if I was mad at him for not staying? I was not and I really understood his reason for not being there. I said Turbo knew how much you loved him and that's enough.

We said goodbye and I sat down with him a little while and I told the tech that it was time, so if I remember they had given Turbo a sedative to calm him down, so they helped me get Turbo out of the cage and I carried him myself to the room they had waiting for us. They told me to take as much time as I needed and they would check on me periodically. I said thank you and I placed him on the table carefully and covered him up so he would not be cold.

After awhile they opened the door and asked me how I was doing? I looked at her and said I was ready but not really, but it was time. She was so nice she came and said goodbye to Turbo and said the doctor would be right there. It felt like forever but it was not that long and the doctor came in and we talked about Turbo and what was best for him. He said such kind words and asked me if I was ready.

How can you ever be ready for something like this? But God left Turbo in our care to be able to make the decisions that were best for him and give him a wonderful life which I believe we did. I never gave up on his care and it was never, never a burden for me to do so. It was a blessing and an honor to have had in him my life.

I watched him get his shot and saw him start to breathe slower and slower so I began to sing a song I sang to him in the mornings. "When I see your face, there's not a thing that I would change, because your amazing just the way you are." It's a song by Bruno Mars. I kissed his tiny face and I was petting his back, when he took his last breath forever.

I had to stop writing at this time. I sat back and started to cry. I have had such a hard time finishing this story when it came to writing about Turbo's passing. I would just look at the screen and cry, and then turn off the computer and not write about it for months. Then one day it was like God was telling me to finish the story. Even when I would try and put it out of my mind, it would come right back and it just would not let up. I finally got the hint. It was time to finish and allow myself to move on. So, I started to write again.

After Turbo passed, I stayed awhile and could not make myself get up and leave him. But I had to go home and take care of everyone else. As I started to leave the vet's office, they asked me if I was okay to drive. I told them I was fine and got in my car, and I was so overwhelmed with the reality that Turbo was never coming home. Never seeing his wonderful little face and feeling his wet kisses. No more Thanksgiving or Christmas's. No more Turbo.

I had to go to the funeral home and make Turbo's arrangements for cremation. It's just like a person. They have a room for pets and they display certain beautiful wooden boxes or other items you can choose from. I must have looked a mess. My eyes were red and swollen from crying. But they deal with grief every day and treated Turbo and I with so much respect. I ended up with a beautiful wooden box and a container with paw prints to wear or use as a key chain. It was a hard thing to do but I'm so glad they offer these services to people. They told me I could see Turbo before he was cremated, so they said they would call me when I was able to see him. I got in my car and when I pulled in the garage Ted was looking out the back door. I could tell he had been crying. I got out of the car and we both started crying and just hugged each other.

I turned around and saw Ben and Rachel just looking at us, not making a sound. Ben walked up and looked toward the door and I had to walk out of the room. He just sat there looking for Turbo. Rachel went in the living room and she laid on her spot, not a sound, the house was quiet.

I started to get them fed and started to get Turbos shot ready… and well, I could not help it. But I got everyone to the point of full belly's and then I went about the usual evening routine. I tried to be as normal as we could be. Ben still slept in his own spot. He didn't try to sleep where Turbo slept until months later.

The funeral home called and said I could come and see Turbo, so after work I went over and I was so happy when I saw the same man who took care of Buster. It was like Buster was taking care of Turbo. He walked me back to where he was going to be cremated and as I came around the corner, I saw Turbo on the table with a blanket wrapped around him. I just looked at him and I kissed his nose and it may sound crazy, but at that moment I knew he was gone. I told him to look for Buster, he would be waiting for him. And kissed him one last time. When it was time for the cremation I left.

A few days went by and I was looking in a newspaper and glanced at the obituaries and I thought why not do that for Turbo? So, I got in touch with our local newspaper and they said it would not be a problem. I didn't tell Ted because I wanted to surprise him. I found a picture I loved of Turbo and wrote up his obituary and placed it in the Sunday paper.

Ted always gets the Sunday paper and I told him to look at this ad I saw and I wanted his opinion. When he saw Turbos obituary he smiled and was crying at the same time. I told him it was not meant to hurt him, but a way to honor Turbo because he was a family member and should have his notice of passing too.

Ted was very happy-sad, but in a good way. The response from our friends and our clients was so overwhelming. The cards we got were amazing and my family and friends from Facebook even sent cards. It made my heart so happy that Turbo touched so many people's lives too.

I got the call from the Funeral Home that his remains were ready to be picked up. I thought I was okay until I walked in their front door and they gave there condolence's again and I said thank you. I took the nice bag the ashes were in and sat in my car, crying. It was so hard for me not to look inside but I wanted to wait and open it with Ted. When I got home, we sat down to look inside and there as a lock of his hair in a pretty blue bag and his paw print and noise print on his Certificate of Cremation.

Wow it was beautiful the way it was placed and presented so I put it on the shelf next to Buster and now I have Turbo home. It was hard to adjust to Turbo being gone. I would still wake up three times a night looking for him to put on the bed and take off the bed. Sometimes I would even find myself getting his pills or shot's ready. But I know he's in a better place and I know someday I will see him and Buster again.

Here is the Obituary on Turbo. I hope you like it.

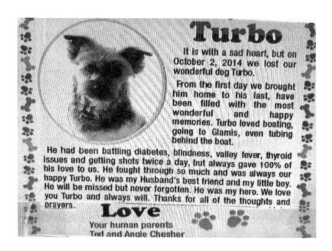

Turbo

It is with a sad heart, but on October 2, 2014 we lost our wonderful dog Turbo.

From the first day we brought him home to his last, have been filled with the most wonderful and happy memories. Turbo loved boating, going to Glamis, even tubing behind the boat.

He had been battling diabetes, blindness, valley fever, thyroid issues and getting shots twice a day, but always gave 100% of his love to us. He fought through so much and was always our happy Turbo. He was my Husband's best friend and my little boy. He will be missed but never forgotten. He was my hero. We love you Turbo and always will. Thanks for all of the thoughts and prayers.

Love

Your human parents
Ted and Angie Chesher

It has taken me almost three and a half years to even write this story. Every time I got to the part of Turbos passing, I could not get myself to finish it. I would start crying and would just stop and walk away. But I have learned something from doing this... time does heal. It may sound silly, corny, or hokey to some, but it's true for me. I can now write things down and remember the memories of Turbo and smile and think what a wonderful dog he was and what a blessing he was in our lives.

At one point I just couldn't bring myself to finish this story and it sat haunting me. I would say I even felt a nudge now and then from God to sit down and finish Turbo's story, but I have to say I pretty much ignored his voice this time. Then one day, Ted was cleaning our swimming pool and there was a small bird floating in it. Its wing was hurt but Ted set it down to check it and let it dry out. It was still alive so we put him in the neighbor's little bird house to let him recover and keep him safe from predators.

When I checked on him and gave him some water and a piece of bread, he didn't look like he would be able to fly again. I thought if he wasn't better by the next morning, I would take him to a wild animal rescuer here in Lake Havasu. But when I got up the next day he was gone. I thought the worst. Some animal must have attacked the poor thing because he couldn't get away. That week had been a rough week and I still was fighting God's nudge to finish this story.

Sitting at my desk that day, a little bird landed on my porch railing and sat there looking at me and chirping happily. I was sure it was our little injured bird as his wing was still damaged. I thanked God for protecting this little guy. I also knew in my heart that God was telling me just as he had taken care of this creature of his, he was taking care of our Turbo. So, I sat down at my computer and I began writing the final chapters of this story.

Is there a tear that still flows down my cheek every now and then? YES, YES, YES. I will never forget any of my pets, but I have come to understand they are in a better place with no pain and I can only imagine how beautiful heaven is. But knowing they are there makes it so much easier and makes me very happy in my heart. Some people may not believe animals go to heaven, but I believe they do. God made these beautiful animals and the wonderful things they do for us. I believe they are rewarded for their unconditional love and companionship and saving our lives with their support and comfort. That's more than a lot of people can give of themselves.

I hope you can see it's a lot of work to have a pet, so when you think you want one, please look at the big picture. Can I afford the food or the health care? If they get sick can I take care of them? It's so easy to fall in love with a pet. I am guilty myself of having those feelings in the past, but if I couldn't continue to care for them, I always found them a loving home. They deserve that much from all of us.

We all have had issues that were not foreseeable but there are so many organizations and people out there to help you. So, if you can't take care of them, please take them to your local animal shelter and give them a chance at life. I was blessed with a good vet and a place where I could get Turbo's insulin at a low cost. So please, love and respect your pet every day, they do that for you.

It's with a very sad heart, but while I was writing this story, we lost our beautiful Rachel. She got sick and we lost her very quickly, within a couple of weeks. I'm just very thankful for the care of her vet and his wife for the dignity she was given when I had to say goodbye for the last time. I stayed with her and sang to her and loved her till her last breath.

I saw her before her cremation, they had her in a room and I spent a long time with her. Rachel was not a touchy-feely kind of dog when she was alive, so now I had a chance to hug her and kiss her to my heart's content. But when I finally started to walk away, I started crying again and went back in for one last kiss on her cute nose.

Rest in peace Rachel May 18th 2016

Maggie

With a very sad heart we said goodbye to our Maggie
Mae Chesher on Friday March 1, 2019.

It was a blessing to me that as I kissed her and said I
loved her, she passed away in my arms. I will always
remember the day I met her in a shelter and I asked to
see the beautiful gray and white kitty with green eyes.
When they opened her cage door, her little arms
wrapped around my neck and it was love at first sight.
God blessed us the day we found each other and she
will be forever in my heart. We love you Maggie Mae,
your human parents and your doggie brother Ben.

I'm sitting here looking out the window at the beautiful blue sky and the sun is so bright and warm. I am thanking God for all of the blessings in my life. I looked down at Ben sitting with me in my chair and it's amazing how much I love him. I don't know what I would have done if I didn't have him when I lost my Turbo, Rachel, and Maggie. I used to wonder what was my purpose in life? So many wonderful people do such wonderful things: singing, speaking, healing, writing, teaching. And this is what I have come up with.

The people I have met, good or bad, have all been a tool to help me learn to be wiser. I listen a lot better, forgive much easier, don't judge and place my trust in God. He will help me with everything I need if I just listen for his voice. Life is so unpredictable; it really is true… we should live and love everyday like it's our last day on earth.

I realize looking back and having learned from getting older, and growing in my walk with God, that I had to go through everything in my life to get where I am today. If I didn't, I wouldn't have met Ted and the journey that got us to where we are today. Some people may also think that the journey with Turbo was insignificant, but to me it defined my life.

God used Turbo to reveal His strength, patience and unconditional love to me in a personal way. It isn't as if my life hadn't been given examples of His love all along my journey. But it took all the little miracles God revealed with Turbo to make me finally see His daily provision in my life. I could look back now and see all the times He had brought me through trials. Now there is not a day that I am not grateful and thankful for all His blessings.

I believe Turbo and I were meant to be in each other's lives and because of Turbo we got Rachel and Ben. Would I do it all again? Yes, I would because the thought of never having Turbo in our lives makes life seem so small. Thank you, Turbo, for enriching our lives, because of you the love continues on for Ben and Ted and I and all the wonderful memories we have are because you brought us all together. Turbo you are my hero and will be forever in my heart. We love you, your human parents.

Love, Angie and Ted.

For
the
Love
of
Turbo

Made in the USA
Las Vegas, NV
25 June 2021